SPITFIRE

THE LEGEND LIVES ON

SPITFIRE

THE LEGEND LIVES ON

Jeremy Flack

Published in 1992 by
Osprey Publishing Limited
59 Grosvenor Street, London W1X 9DA

ISBN 1855321963

Editor Dennis Baldry
Photography Jeremy Flack
Text Mike Jerram
Page design Colin Paine
Printed in Hong Kong

Front cover There will always be an
England ... while there is a country
lane, a patchwork of fields and a
Spitfire dancing through the clouds —
in this case the RAF Battle of Britain
Memorial Flight's Griffon-engined
PR Mk XIX

Back cover Break! Break! Old Flying
Machine Company pilot Brian Smith
rolls Spitfire HF Mk IX MH434,
resplendent in Belgian Air Force
markings for the 1991 airshow
season

Title page Elliptical elegance.
American David Pennell's newly-
restored Spitfire HF Mk IXE displays
Supermarine designer R J Mitchell's
classic wing shape

For a catalogue of all books published by Osprey Aerospace
please write to:

**The Marketing Department, Octopus Illustrated Books,
1st Floor, Michelin House, 81 Fulham Road, London SW3 6RB**

Stephen Grey, from the Fighter Collection, waves chocks
away at the start of another sortie in his clip-wing Spitfire
LF Mk IXE ML417

Introduction

'When the 50th anniversary of the Battle of Britain is celebrated in 1990, there will be even more Spitfires in the air than today. Another generation will hear the sound of freedom and see one of the world's best loved aeroplanes'. Those words appeared at the end of the introduction to *Spitfire – A Living Legend*, Jeremy Flack's first pictorial tribute to Britain's most celebrated fighter which was published in 1985.

The fact that *Spitfire – The Legend Lives On* is a completely new book reflects the relentless growth of the Spitfire restoration scene. 'Old friends' from the RAF Battle of Britain Memorial Flight qualify for inclusion as of right, but many of their Spitfires have been repainted in new squadron markings since the original book was published.

Without the generous cooperation of the many restorers, engineers, pilots and organizers named in this book – not forgetting the substantial level of support from the BBMF – this book would be full of blank pages. Operating warbirds is an expensive, time-consuming business, and photography – especially the air-to-air variety – has to be fitted in at the discretion of the owner/pilot/operator, often at very short notice when a 'target of opportunity' arises. To everyone who helped, a thousand thanks.

With his wife Julie, Jeremy Flack runs Aviation Photographs International (API), a Swindon-based company launched in 1969. API is able to rapidly supply a wide range of high quality transparencies on air force, navy and army subjects – from stock, or to order as required. Jeremy Flack uses Canon cameras and lenses, loaded with Fuji and Kodachrome.

Right Relegated to ground duties as long ago as 1954 and stuck on a pole outside RAF Uxbridge for 15 years, Spitfire LF Mk XVIE RW382 returned to its natural element in 1991 after a faultless rebuild by Historic Flying Limited

Contents

Introduction

'First of the Few'   8

Up where they belong   20

Better than new   62

Spit and polish   88

Spit personalities   119

'First of the Few'

5 March 1936. The prototype Supermarine Type 300 K5054, as yet unnamed, awaits its first flight from the Supermarine Aviation Works at Eastleigh Airport near Southampton ... Not quite. 55 years separate this photograph from the day Reginald Mitchell's masterpiece took to the air, for this is Clive du Cros's magnificent full-scale replica of the first Spitfire, awaiting *its* maiden flight in the summer of 1991 at RAF Hullavington in Wiltshire

Right and opposite Unlike the original, du Cros's prototype Spitfire is made entirely from wood, a douglas fir and sitka spruce airframe skinned with birch ply, but is otherwise faithful to the clean unspoilt lines of the original

No Merlin this, but a Jaguar V-12 automobile engine with modified fuel and oil systems and dual ignition. Capacity has been increased to six litres, enabling the engine to put out 350 hp via a custom-built reduction gearbox. The Type 300's Merlin C produced close to its design power output of 1000 hp

Clive, son Christian and many willing helpers were on hand to move the replica from its workshop in Swindon to the gliding club hangar at RAF Hullavington where final assembly took place

With most systems installed, first engine runs were made on 13 February 1990, followed by 25 hours of ground trials which included high speed runs down Hullavington's main runway. The silver dope paint scheme of du Cros's replica duplicates the natural metal and primer finish in which the real K5054 made its initial flight before being given a high gloss finish of Supermarine Seaplane Enamel, the precise bluish-grey shade of which is the subject of endless debate among latter-day researchers

Once preliminary trials of the Jaguar V-12 were satisfactorily completed, Clive was ready to install the Spitfire's close-fitting cowling panels. Slotted wheel hubs, large underwing radiator fairing, round rather than oval exhaust ports and (not seen here) a tailwheel rather than a skid are concessions to total authenticity, but lack of undercarriage leg fairings is correct – they were not fitted to K5054 until after its first flight

Above Test pilot Pete Thorn studies the instrument panel layout with engineer Nick Pearson prior to the first flight. Although the basic flight instruments are identical to those of the original Spitfire, engine gauges reflect the Jaguar's automobile ancestry

Right She flies! Pete Thorn lifts the 'second' K5054 off Hullavington's runway on 7 June 1991, two days after the 55th anniversary of the original's maiden flight, and the culmination of 10 years' hard work for Clive du Cros and his team. Apocryphal story has it that after Vickers test pilot 'Mutt' Summers flew the type 300 for just 15 minutes on that day in 1936 he declared it perfect, a real 'flies off the drawing board' aeroplane. Of such stuff are legends made, but, alas, rarely are they true. Summers' protégé Jeffrey Quill, who was at Eastleigh for the first flight and, after Summers' retirement, became the doyen of Spitfire test pilots, recalls that what Summers actually said to designer Reginald Mitchell was that he didn't want anything touched or altered until he had a chance to fly K5054 again and assess it more thoroughly – not quite the same thing. Mitchell never lived to see the Spitfire enter service or develop through its myriad of different versions far removed from the design he had conceived; he died of stomach cancer a year after K5054 flew. Nor did the prototype last long. Brought up to production Mk I standard, it overturned on landing, killing its pilot, at Farnborough on 4 September 1939 – the day after war was declared. The historic airframe, which had logged just over 151 flying hours, was briefly used as a mock-up for photo reconnaissance camera installations and then scrapped

Up where they belong

These pages and overleaf Closer ... closer ... hold it! Sqn Ldr Paul Day, AFC, Fighter Leader of the RAF's Battle of Britain Memorial Flight, tucks Spitfire PR Mk XIX PM631 ever tighter into the lens. One of three PR Mk XIXs in the BBMF's collection of five Spitfires, PM631 is the only one not to have seen wartime service. Built at Reading in late 1945, it spent most of its early years with Maintenance Units before joining the Meteorological Research Flight at Hooton Park in 1951, and was a founder member of the BBMF when it formed at RAF Biggin Hill in July 1957. On the Flight's strength ever since, PM631 spent some time at RAF Binbrook in 1963 in the unlikely role of dissimilar air combat 'aggressor', flying against English Electric Lightnings of the Central Fighter Establishment at a time when it was thought possible that RAF Lightnings might be pitted against North American P-51D Mustangs during the Indonesian Confrontation

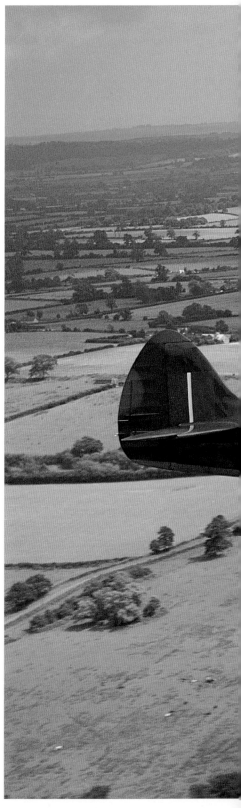

Above Then, and now. In 1985 AVM Ken Hayr, AOC No 11 Group, Strike Command, came up with the novel idea of teaming one of the RAF's oldest fighters with its latest interceptor for a unique airshow routine. Fortuitously No 229 OCU, then converting onto the Panavia F.2 Tornado, and the Battle of Britain Memorial Flight, shared a common base at RAF Coningsby, Lincolnshire. Here Sqn Ldr Paul Day, himself a No 229 OCU instructor, leads the 'Spitnado' duo in PM631 while Wg Cdr Rick Peacock-Edwards holds station in the F.2, wings at full forward sweep and slats extended

Right Photo reconnaissance was an important role for Spitfires during World War 2. The PR Mk XIX was the last of the PR marks, combining the high back fuselage, 2035 hp Rolls-Royce Griffon 66 engine and tail surfaces of the FR Mk XIV, modified PR Mk XI wings and its universal camera installation, and the pressurised cockpit of the PR Mk X. It had a maximum speed of 445 mph at 26,000 feet, a service ceiling of more than 42,000 feet and, with internal fuel capacity of 252 gallons (treble that of the Battle of Britain era Mk I) and 90- or 170-gallon drop tanks, could range more than 1400 miles. A total of 225 PR Mk XIXs were built. After World War 2 the Swedish Air Force purchased 50 PR Mk XIXs, while others went to India and Thailand. Here PM631 wears late war camouflage and black-and-white invasion stripes to masquerade as Mk XIV DL-E of No 91 Sqn for the 40th anniversary of the D-Day landings in 1984

Preceding pages Puffy white clouds and a Spitfire in which to chase them. What more could any man ask?

These pages Gleaming in the high gloss PRU Blue finish it wore while serving with No 16 Sqn, 2nd Tactical Air Force in 1945, PS853 is another of the Battle of Britain Memorial Flight's trio of Spitfire PR Mk XIXs. Built at Supermarine's Southampton works, it entered service with the Central Photographic Reconnaissance unit at RAF Benson, Oxfordshire in January 1945 and saw action with 2TAF in Belgium, the Netherlands and Germany. Like BBMF companions PM631 and PS915, '853 ended its active service with the celebrated Met Flight at Hooton Park and RAF Woodvale on THUM (Temperature and Humidity) duties, and made the RAF' last ever Spitfire operational sortie on 9 June 1957, following which the THUM task was taken over by DH Mosquitoes. Four days later Group Captain Johnnie Johnson ferried the aircraft to Biggin Hill to join the newly established Memorial Flight. PS853 was later placed 'on the gate' at Central Fighter Establishment, RAF West Raynham, before restoration to airworthiness for the BBMF in 1964

Shot from the tail-gunner's turret of the BBMF's flagship Avro Lancaster *City of Lincoln*, PR Mk XIX PS853 leads the Flight's Hawker Hurricane IIC LF363, which was the last Hurricane to enter RAF service. Ironically Sqn Ldr Allan Martin, at the helm of PS853 on this occasion, was flying the Hurricane in September 1991 when it suffered an inflight engine failure while en route from the Flight's base at RAF Coningsby to Jersey for a Battle of Britain Week display. Despite Sqn Ldr Martin's skill in making a very rapid wheels-up emergency landing at RAF Wittering, fire quickly consumed the historic airframe. Though not completely destroyed, its future is uncertain

Full frontal. PS853's Griffon 66 ran out of hours in 1984. With no replacement to be had, the Flight, in conjunction with Rolls-Royce, engineered a conversion to enable the more plentiful Griffon 58 from Avro Shackletons to be installed. It flew again, externally unchanged but with much internal redesign and modification, in July 1989

Above and overleaf Affectionately known to BBMF members as 'Baby', Mk IIA
P7350 was the 14th of 11,939 Spitfires built at Vickers-Armstrong's 'shadow'
Castle Bromwich Aircraft Factory (CBAF) near Birmingham. Entering service
with No 266 (Rhodesia) Sqn at RAF Wittering on 6 September 1940, it later
served with Nos 603 (City of Edinburgh), 616 (County of South Yorkshire) and
64 Sqn and with the Central Gunnery School at RAF Sutton Bridge, and is
credited with having destroyed three enemy aircraft (not entirely unscathed –
BBMF maintenance staff say you can still see bullet hole repair patches in its
skin). Repaired three times after suffering Category B damage in flying
accidents, P7350 ended its service days with 39 Maintenance Unit at RAF
Colerne, where it was sold as scrap for £25. Fortunately the scrap dealer
realised the historic value of the aircraft and re-presented it to the station as a
museum piece. Restored in 1968, like many other Spitfires, for a role in the epic
movie *The Battle of Britain*, the rare Mk IIA was presented to the Battle of
Britain Memorial Flight after filming was completed, and is shown here wearing
its 1985/86 season colours as presentation aircraft *Observer Corps* EB-Z of
No 41 Sqn

Aloft from its long-time base at Booker (Wycombe Air Park) is Spitfire Mk IA AR213/G-AIST, which was built by Westland Aircraft at Yeovil in the summer of 1941 as part of a mixed batch of Mks I and V. Already outmoded by later marks, AR213 spent an uneventful war with Operational Training Units and was sold in 1947, along with a Mk V, to Grp Capt (later Air Commodore) Allen Wheeler, and stored unflown with the Shuttleworth Trust at Old Warden Aerodrome until returned to airworthiness as one of the many Spitfire stars of *The Battle of Britain.* The late Hon Patrick Lindsay acquired AR213 and had it maintained in immaculate condition by Personal Plane Services at Booker, whose managing director Tony Bianchi is seen here flying it for current owner Victor Gauntlett, chairman of Proteus Petroleum and a stalwart supporter of historic aircraft preservation and aerobatics in the UK

With her cowling already stained by the exhaust from the Jaguar V-12
powerplant, Clive du Cros's replica of Spitfire prototype K5054 cruises serenely
over the English countryside. Pilot Pete Thorn has slid the canopy back to get a
better view of Jeremy Flack's cameraship

Left Them and us. The late Charles Church in his two-seat Spitfire Tr9 PT462/G-CTIX leads his Spanish-built Hispano HA. 1112-M1L Buchon G-HUNN, Swiss Pilatus P-2 G-CJCI – both imitating Messerschmitt Bf 109s with varing degrees of success – and P-51D Mustang G-SUSY on a sortie from his base at Popham, Hampshire

Opposite Church's Tr9 started life at Castle Bromwich as a single-seat HF Mk IX. After service with the Mediterranean Allied Air Force it was sold post-war to the Italian Air Force and moved on in 1952 to the Israeli Air Force. Little is known of its career there, but in the early 1980s the partially buried remains of the aircraft were discovered on a kibbutz by British warbirds enthusiast Robs Lamplough and brought back to their homeland after an absence of nearly 40 years. Acquired by Charles Church (Spitfires) Ltd in 1985, PT462 was rebuilt to Supermarine Type 509 Mk 9 Spitfire Trainer configuration by engineer Dick Melton, and flew again for the first time on 25 July 1987 in the hands of Shuttleworth Collection chief pilot John Lewis. Between 1948–51 Vickers converted 20 surplus Mk IX Spitfires to Tr9 standard for export – three for the Dutch Air Force, 10 for the Indian Air Force, one for Egypt and six for the Irish Air Corps

Another D-Day veteran is Tr9 ML407/G-LFIX, which shared the Castle Bromwich line with ML417 in 1944. Flown by pilots of No 485 (Royal New Zealand Air Force) Sqn, it completed 69 fighter-bomber sweeps, 30 Normandy beach-head patrols and six armed reconnaissance sorties during the Allied landings. It accounted for two Junkers Ju 88s (one shared) and two Bf 109s downed and one damaged, one of the Ju 88s being shot down by its regular pilot F/O Johnnie Houlton over Omaha Beach on D-Day itself. ML407 served with six RNZAF, Polish, Free French and Norwegian squadrons of the 2nd Tactical Air Force in Normandy and Belgium, and was converted into a Tr9 trainer during 1951 for the Irish Air Corps. Acquired by Samuelson Films in 1968 as a back-up airframe for the film *The Battle of Britain* and later sold to the Strathallan Collection in Scotland, ML407 was bought in August 1979 by the late Nick Grace, and moved to his workshops in St Merryn, Cornwall, where he undertook a remarkable six-year rebuild with the help of former BBMF engineer Dick Melton. Flown again by Grace himself on 16 April 1985, ML407 incorporated some non-standard modifications during its reconstruction, including a lowered rear canopy with transparent 'tunnel' between the cockpits, and 'wet wing' fuel cells which increase capacity from 25 to 60 gallons per wing. Painted once again as a OU-V of No 485 (RNZAF) Sqn, ML407 was the centrepiece of a nostalgic re-union at St Just Aerodrome, Cornwall shortly after its re-birth when three of its former pilots, including Johnnie Houlton were re-united with their old mount

These pages and overleaf Another escapee from dereliction in Israel is Spitfire HF Mk IXE MJ730/G-BLAS, rescued by Robs Lamplough in 1979 and restored by Guy Black and Steve Atkins of Aero Vintage, and Trent Aero at East Midlands Airport. It is seen here aloft on a test flight from EMA in November 1988 with Rolls-Royce PLC's Dave Moore at the controls, painted as No 249 Sqn's GN-F for then owner American Fred Smith

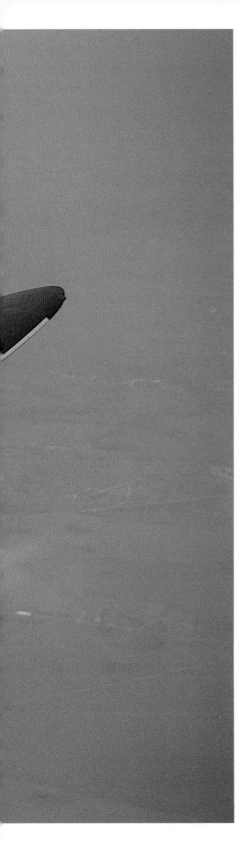

Left Fred Smith never did take MJ730 across the Atlantic, but sold it in the UK to David Pennell. He chose a new colour scheme representing a presentation aircraft of No 154 Sqn, whose Spitfire Mk IXs operated in the Mediterranean during 1943/44

Above MJ730 correctly shows No 154 Sqn's badge – three arrows and a 'derestriction' road sign – but its motto is properly *His modis ad victoriam* (this way to victory). As classics students will know. *Nil illegitimae carborundum* means something entirely different

The Old Flying Machine Company's MH434/G-ASJV is perhaps the best known of all restored Spitfires thanks to exuberant airshow displays by the late Neil Williams and Ray Hanna (whose son Mark is at the controls here), and for the then record price of £260,000 paid for it at Christie's Duxford auction in 1983. MH434 is of 1943-vintage, built originally as a clip-wing LF Mk IX, but now in HF Mk IX guise with the two 20 mm cannon, four .303 Browning machine gun 'B' wing. Derived from the Spitfire Mk V to take advantage of the increased power available from the two-stage, two-speed supercharger Merlin 60-series engine, the Mk IX was developed in 1942 to counter the threat of the *Luftwaffe's* Fw 190 and was 70 mph faster than the Mk V, with a 10,000 foot increase in service ceiling. The Mark IX was the most-produced mark of Spitfire, with 5663 built, and to many pilots the best-handling of all

These pages and overleaf MH434 has a combat history. Flying this aircraft from RAF Hornchurch with No 222 (Natal) Sqn, Flt Lt H P Lardner-Burke, DFC shot down one Fw 190 and damaged another on 27 August 1943 while accompanying USAAF B-17 Fortresses on 'Ramrod' daylight escort duties, and brought down another Fw 190 and shared a Bf 109F the following month. After war service MH434 was sold to the Royal Netherlands Air Force and served in Indonesia before returning to Europe with the Belgian Air Force in 1953. On this photo sortie, flown by OFMC pilot Brian Smith, the aircraft had been painted in Belgian Air Force markings for the 1991 airshow season, when it took part in celebrations at the Biggin Hill Air Fair to mark the daring escape from Nazi-occupied Belgium in July 1941 of Lieutenant General Aviateur Baron 'Mike' Donnet, DFC. The code letters CK-D are spurious, a left-over from filming the television series *A Perfect Hero* during the previous year

Above MT719/I-SPIT wouldn't have found the grass so green and the
buttercups so yellow when on wartime service with No 17 Sqn operating out o
Vavuyina and China Bay during the Burma Campaign, commemorated by its
SEAC camouflage scheme. This Southampton-built LF Mk VIIIC stayed in the
East, joining the Indian Air Force at war's end, and was bought in 1978 by the
late Ormond Hayden-Baillie and his brother Wensley. Passed on to Italian
warbird enthusiast Franco Actis, it was restored in Turin by former BBMF
technicians Paul Mercer, 'Kick' Houltby and Pete Rushen, who installed a 1740
hp Merlin 114A engine from a Mosquito in place of its corroded Merlin 66, and
replaced some 90 per cent of its magnesium rivets during a four-year rebuild.
The BBMF's Sqn Ldr Paul Day performed the first flight from SIAI-Marchetti's
airfield at Vergiate on 27 October 1982. I-SPIT is now back in Britain in the
hands of Aircraft Investments and is maintained by Dick Melton. It is still
appropriately registered as G-VIII

Better than new

These pages and overleaf In deepest Hampshire, not far from the Spitfire's Southampton birthplace and the numerous dispersal sites, mostly garages, in which components for some 8000 Spitfires were built in wartime, is the new 'Spitfire factory' set up by the late Charles Church and now operated by Dick Melton Aviation. In these views can be seen the camouflaged nose of Church's restored Tr9 PT462/GCTIX, and in yellow-etch primer finish his clip-wing LF Mk IXE PL344/G-IXCC, which saw active service with a number of 2nd TAF units during the Allied advance across occupied Europe in 1944/45. Left behind in the Netherlands at war's end to become an instructional airframe with the Anthony Fokker Technical School, it was retrieved by Charles Church (Spitfires) Ltd in 1985, and flew again after rebuild on 11 March 1991. Awaiting attention among the roof beams is the fuselage of former Indian Air Force Spitfire F Mk XIV SM832/G-WWII. Hurricane G-ORGI, undergoing the finishing touches to its rebuild by Paul Mercer when these pictures were taken, took to the air again on 8 September 1991, completing a busy year for Dick Melton Aviation

Above Dick Melton is also building up a post-production 509 Series Spitfire Trainer from newly fabricated components. When completed, it will be the 20,352nd Spitfire built

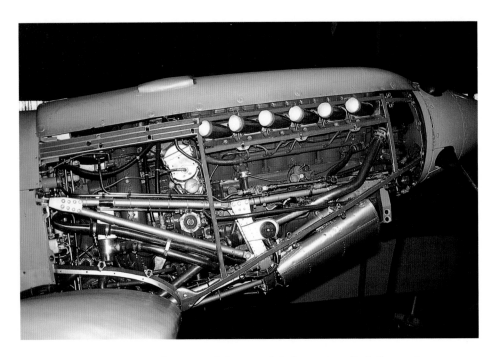

Above MJ627 now has an ex-Mosquito Merlin 76 installed; the engine ran again after rebuild on 18 March 1990

Right Almost there. Maurice Bayliss has been working on the restoration of his Spitfire Tr9 MJ627/G-BMSB since 1978. Built as an LF Mk IX at Castle Bromwich at the end of 1943, it was converted into a trainer for the Irish Air Corps eight years later. Following retirement and a spell of duty as an instructional airframe it came back to England in 1963 but found no takers when advertised for sale in *Flight International* at £1500! It was later bought for spares by the then owner of The Old Flying Machine Company's MH434/G-ASJV

Above Although one-off two-seat Spitfire conversions were carried out in the field by No 261 Sqn in Sicily and in Russia during World War 2, Vickers did not create a trainer variant of the fighter until 1946 when Mk VIII MT818 was rebuilt as the sole T Mk VIII N32/G-AIDN, which still survives in the United States. From it developed the tandem-seating Tr9 conversion which involved moving the front cockpit forward by 13½ inches and adding a second cockpit behind, raised slightly to give the back-seater a reasonable forward view. Maurice Bayliss's Tr9 retains the Vickers canopy arrangement, which may be compared with ML407/G-LFIX's low-profile canopy and transparent inter-cockpit 'tunnel' illustrated in the previous chapter

Right and overleaf Being test flown by Mike Searle following rebuild by Trent Aero at East Midlands Airport is Warbirds of Great Britain's Spitfire LF Mk XVIE TE356/G-SXVI, one of a growing number of former RAF gate guardians to take to the air again. Delivered too late for wartime service, TE356 was downgraded to instructional airframe status in 1952 and spent 15 years on RAF Bicester's parade ground before Hollywood beckoned and it joined the non-flying 'extras' used in filming *The Battle of Britain*. Periods of 'pole sitting' outside the Central Flying School establishments at RAF Kemble, RAF Little Rissington and the RAF College at Cranwell followed. WoGB's Doug Arnold obtained the Spitfire in 1986 in trade for an ex-Yugoslav Air Force Republic P-47D Thunderbolt destined for the RAF Museum at Hendon. As G-SXVI the LF Mk XVIE flew again for the first time on 16 December 1987

Above G-CDAN is also an LF Mk XVIE, a 'high-back' example this time. During service with No 17 Sqn at RAF Chivenor it appeared at the 1950 Farnborough Air Show (none too convincingly) disguised as a Messerschmitt Bf 109 for a Battle of Britain commemorative set-piece. Five years later it was in the hands of Metro-Goldwyn-Meyer as a 'prop' for filming cockpit scenes of *Reach for the Sky*, and later served as a source of spares for aircraft used in making *The Battle of Britain*. After many years of storage it was acquired by The Fighter Collection at Duxford. Stephen Grey is seen here giving the aircraft an air test in the autumn of 1988 prior to dismantling and shipping it to new owner Tim Wallis in New Zealand. Damaged in a landing accident shortly after arrival, it has since been rebuilt once more and now flies in original clip-winged configuration from Wanaka as TB863/ZK-XVI

Right and below Dave Lees of The Fighter Collection at work on FR Mk XIV MV293/G-SPIT, one of a batch of ex-Indian Air Force aircraft retrieved by Doug Arnold of Warbirds of Great Britain

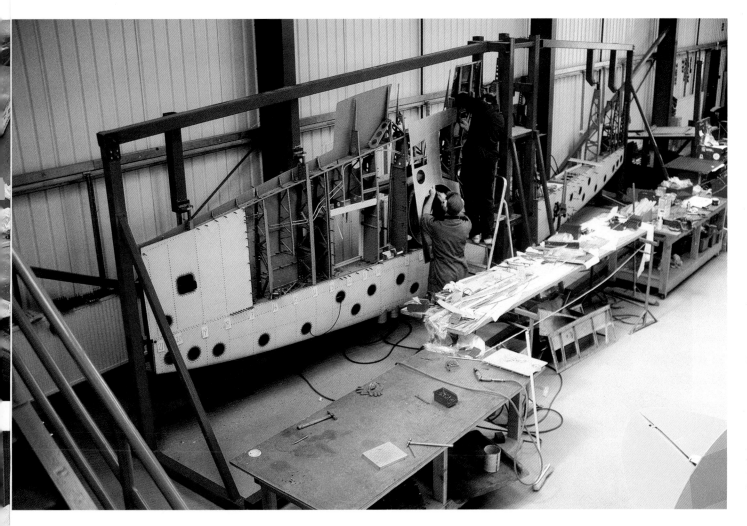

Above Tim Routsis and Clive Denney have set up a veritable Spitfire production line at their Historic Flying Limited facility at Audley End. Here staff work on re-skinning the jigged wing of Spitfire LF Mk XVIE TD248/G-OXVI, which will become the second former gate guardian to be returned to airworthiness by HF when it flies again in 1992. Pretty though it was, the Spitfire's airframe, with its elegant ellipses and curves, was ill-suited to wartime mass-production methods and took much longer to manufacture than the simpler, biplane-era structure of the Hurricane

Each of the Battle of Britain Memorial Flight's aircraft has fresh unit markings applied during a major service. Spitfire PR Mk XIX PM631, seen in the previous chapter wearing D-Day colours, now carries the blue and white roundels and name *Mary* of a Mk XIV of No 11 Sqn while serving with South East Asia Command in the summer of 1945. Pictured in the BBMF hangar at RAF Coningsby, PM631 has its cowlings removed, revealing that, like stablemate PS853, it too now flies on an ex-Shackleton Griffon 58 engine

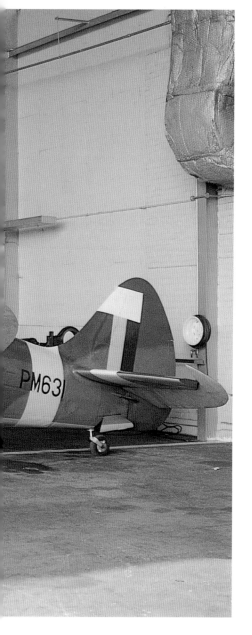

Above Historic Flying's Tim Routsis (left) and Martin Henocq shed some light on a problem with the main undercarriage legs of TD248

David Pennell's HF Mk IXE MJ730/G-BLAS has now lost its No 154 Sqn colours and reappeared with No 32 Sqn's hunting horn crest as GZ-? *The CO's Query*. The original GZ-? was a Spitfire F Mk XVIII based on the island of Cyprus in 1949

Below Then . . . Spitfire LF Mk XVIE TD248 on gate duty at RAF Sealand in 1984 when it wore the DW-A code letters of No 610 (County of Chester) Sqn, Royal Auxiliary Air Force (see overleaf)

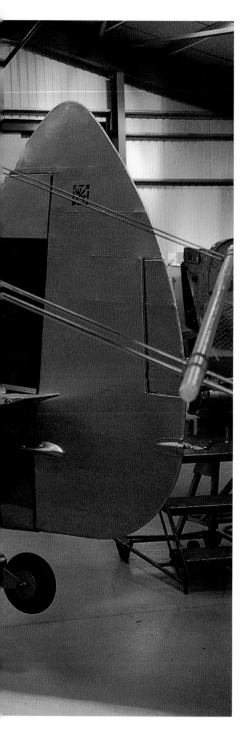

Above Whether No 41 Sqn painted their engine blocks red and polished their rocker covers history does not record, but that's how Mike Nixon of California-based Vintage V-12s finished this immaculate rebuilt Packard Merlin 266 for TD248

Left ... and now, in Historic Flying's workshop in October 1991, well on the way to completion for owner Eddie Coventry, Chairman of BAC Windows and an enthusiastic air racing pilot and sport flying sponsor. Improbable though it looks, that shiny paint job created in HF's integral spray/bake unit *is* authentic: No 41 Sqn's Spitfire F.21s wore a similar scheme when based at RAF Wittering in 1946

David Tallichet's LF Mk XVIE RW382 (see Chapter 2) seen at RAF Uxbridge before retrieval by Historic Flying, and being prepared in the Audley End hangar prior to its first flight on 3 July 1991. The biplane to the rear of Eddie Coventry's silver and red Spitfire is the late Peter Treadaway's Naval Aircraft Factory N3N-3, a rarity in Europe

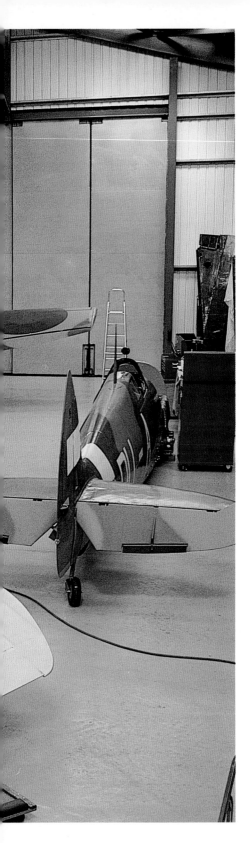

Proving that you never know what lurks behind the crack in a hangar door, this remarkable 1991 Spitfire production line scene, headed by the Tallichet and Coventry Mk XVIEs, with Guy Black's Mk IXE waiting in the wings and Rudy Frasca's Mk XVIIIE bringing up the rear. No, that's not a Spitfire in the foreground, but a Taylor Monoplane homebuilt

Spit and polish

Tail up in classic Spitfire stance, Tony Bianchi gets Victor Gauntlett's Mk IA rolling for take-off at the Biggin Hill Air Fair

Overleaf Perfect planform. The Battle of Britain Memorial Flight's Mk IIA P7350 was restored to its 1940 colours as UO-T of No 266 (Rhodesia) Sqn for the 50th anniversary of the Battle

The late Roland Fraissinet's PR Mk XI PL983 (nearest camera, and now owned by Warbirds of Great Britain), BBMF Mk IIA P7350, and Victor Gauntlett's Mk IA AR213 on the apron at Southampton (Eastleigh) Airport on 5 March 1986 for the 50th anniversary of the prototype Spitfire's first flight from the field. None of these aircraft was Southampton-built

Above BBMF and friends at Coningsby

Right Spitfire spinners. Three- four- and five-blade props lined up at the BBMF base at RAF Coningsby. In the foreground is the late Nick Grace's Tr9 ML407, and towards the rear – and definitely improperly dressed on parade – Spencer Flack's startlingly scarlet FR Mk XIVE G-FIRE/NH904, since sold in the US

Ten (count 'em) airworthy Spitfires and two 'other brands' assembled at the A&AEE Boscombe Down in 1990 for the Royal Air Force Benevolent Fund's Battle of Britain Salute. The BBMF's ill-fated Hurricane LF363 GN-A heads the line-up (right)

Above Spot the interloper. Spitfire and Hurricane flank a Spanish-built Hispano HA.1112-M1L Buchon painted up to represent a Messerschmitt Bf 109. At least it, like its adversaries, is Merlin-powered

Left Tails tell a tail. The early style rudder of The Old Flying Machine Company's MH434 gave way to the broad-chord, pointed-tip type (behind). Later in the Spitfire Mk IX production run, Griffon-engined variants (end of row) had an entirely different fin/rudder shape

Above *Scramble!* A young fighter pilot braves the machine gun fire of a strafing Messerschmitt to get airborne and beat off the attacking Hun. Actually this lad was having his dream of flying in a Spitfire fulfilled by BBC Television's *Jim'll Fix It*, whose director thought the ride in Nick Grace's two-seater would be further enlivened by an airfield attack from Lindsey Walton in his *Emil* look-alike Nord 1002/Messerschmitt Bf 108

Above There are only two kinds of pilot, so the saying goes: those who *have* landed wheels-up, and those who *will* . . . Through no fault of his own, the late Nick Grace joined the former category on (of all days!) 5 March 1986 when ML407's main landing gear legs collapsed as he arrived at Eastleigh Airport for the 50th anniversary celebrations of the Spitfire's first flight. In wartime, landing-gear meant a 'fine' of £5 payable to the repair crew and at least one round of drinks for everyone in the Mess. These days it comes more expensive, but fortunately Nick's rear-seat passenger was his insurance broker, who vouched that the 'chassis' had indeed been selected *down* and confirmed *locked*. Damage was confined to the tips of the Rotol propeller's wooden tips, engine cowlings and underwing radiator housings. *The Perfect Lady*, displaying distinctly *un*ladylike behaviour on this auspicious occasion, was soon up and about again

Right Big friend . . . little friends. Spitfire leaders Ray Hanna and Stephen Grey call the break as they run in on escort duty for a Northwest Airlines Boeing 747 during the 1986 Fighter Meet at North Weald

Enormous Balbos of Warbirds are the trade mark finale of the annual Classic Fighter Show at Duxford. This was the 1991 gathering, led by (what else?) a quintet of Spitfires. How many of the others can you identify?

As an LF Mk IX with No 412 (RCAF) Sqn, 2nd Tactical Air Force in Holland and Germany PV202 was credited with three 'kills' (two Fw 190s and a Bf 109) on 76 sorties. Converted as a trainer for the Irish Air Corps in 1951 it spent nine years flying from Baldonnel and a further eight as a ground instructional airframe before being retrieved in the Great Spitfire Round-Up which preceded the making of *The Battle of Britain*. After several changes of ownership it ended up in the capably restorative hands of Steve Atkins in Sussex, and emerged to fly again as G-TRIX on 23 February 1990, piloted by Peter Kynsey. It was sold after completion to Richard Parker and was captured here at the 1990 Classic Fighter Show at Duxford

These pages and overleaf Unique among airworthy Spitfires is Warbirds of Great Britain's F Mk XVIIIE SM969/G-BRAF, the only surviving flyable example of what is widely regarded as the definitive Griffon-engined variant, and the last Spitfire to retain the classic elliptical wing planform. Only 300 Mk XVIIIEs were built. SM969 was manufactured at Keevil in the summer of 1945, despatched by sea to Karachi in January 1946 and came back to England 18 months later, apparently remaining in its packing crate until sold to the Indian Air Force in 1949. Doug Arnold of WoGB bought the aeroplane from the Indian Government in 1978. It flew again after rebuild on 12 October 1985 in the hands of Rolls-Royce Bristol and Shuttleworth Collection chief pilot John Lewis. Stored once more for several years, it was photographed at the 1991 Cranfield Air Show on a rare public foray from its Biggin Hill base, looking refreshingly 'different' in its all-silver post-war colour scheme and personal D-A 'code' of David Arnold, Doug's son

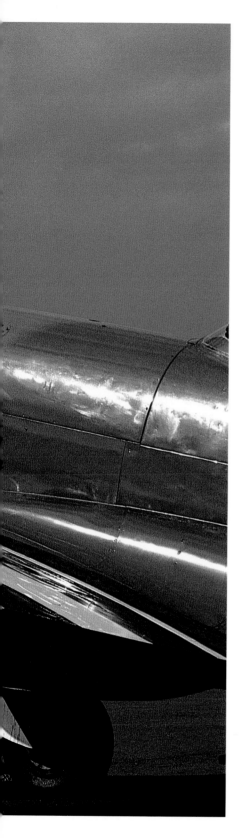

Above Also visiting Duxford, Spitfire F Mk XIVC RM689/G-ALGT, which has been owned since 1950 by engine manufacturer Rolls-Royce. Initially used for Griffon engine development, and later as a chaseplane and high-speed communications aircraft, RM689 is now strictly a showpiece, and a rare example of a manufacturer taking pains to preserve a piece of its own heritage in flying condition. RM689 lives close to Rolls-Royce's Derby headquarters at East Midlands Airport and bears the No 350 (Belgian) Sqn markings worn during service with the 2nd TAF in early 1945

Left Many hands . . . save wear and tear on a BBMF PR Mk XIX's Griffon engine by pulling its five-bladed propeller through to get lubrication flowing before start-up

Keeping a good look out while performing the side-to-side weave which is standard practice when taxying a Spitfire (and most tailwheel warbirds) is Ray Hanna, former leader of the Red Arrows and regarded as *the* Spitfire Maestro by airshow afficionados. MH434 was the foundation stone of Ray and son Mark's Duxford-based Old Flying Machine Company fleet, and is seen here wearing a temporary light grey finish, reminiscent of the high altitude fighter camouflage scheme used on Mk VIIIs and IXs in Italy in 1943/44, for a role in the television series *Poirot*

Making its debut at the 1990 Biggin Hill Air Fair, the Spitfire Formation Aerobatic Team. Building on experience gained while filming the London Weekend Television series *A Piece of Cake*, Ray and Mark Hanna and fellow Old Flying Machine Company pilots Pete Jarvis and Carl Schofield worked up their unique routine flying the OFM's MH434, and Warbirds of Great Britain's LF Mk IXC/E NH238 (on right wing) and PR Mk XI PL983 (left wing). At the time it was thought that no Royal Air Force or any foreign service had ever put on a Spitfire formation aerobatic display in public, making this a unique occasion, but researchers later discovered that the French Air Force had fielded a trio of Mk IXCs as the *Patrouille Tricolore* from the *Ecole de Chasse* at Meknes, Morocco in 1947. Note original rounded rudders of MH434 and NH238, broad-chord pointed-tip style on the PR Mk XI

Spit personalities

A Perfect Lady and a plucky lady. Carolyn Grace about to board Spitfire Tr9 ML407/GLFIX which her husband Nick restored. Tragically, Nick was killed in a car accident in 1988, but Carolyn bravely decided to keep his beloved Spitfire as a tribute to him. Already a licensed pilot, she took dual instruction on it and quickly soloed. On 25 September 1991 Carolyn achieved her ambition when, attending a gathering of women pilots at the invitation of fellow Spitfire owner Victor Gauntlett, she was presented with her Civil Aviation Authority Display Authorisation and performed her first public airshow routine in ML407 in front of an appreciative gathering which included HRH Prince Michael of Kent. The 1992 display season will see many more appearances by this unique duo

Above Dave Moore's 'day job' is flying Rolls-Royce's communications aircraft on company business, but can't you tell that he needs little persuading to spend his weekends in the 'office' of RM689

Left 'There I was ...' AVM Johnnie Johnson, CB, CBE, DSO, DFC, DL, who flew Spitfire Mks I, II, V, IX ('the best Spitfire ever'), XII and XIVs and was credited with 38 victories, swaps stories with Rolls-Royce's Dave Moore in front of R-R's F XIVC

Resting on the backbone of Spitfire HF Mk IXE MJ730/G-BLAS, Trent Aero's Alan Purdy chats with the aircraft's owner David Pennell. Purdy is Trent's Spitfire Coordinator and Chief Engineer, and has been responsible for restoring four of the breed and an additional eight sets of wings in the company's East Midlands Airport workshops. He's currently engaged in rebuilding a Seafire

Below Prototype team. Assembled in front of the magnificent Supermarine Type 300 replica are (left to right): retired Vickers-Armstrong senior inspector Len Morris, who received CAA authorisation to carry out airframe inspections during construction; Ray Hilbourn, who undertook structural stressing; owner/builder Clive du Cros, and test pilot Pete Thorn

The Fighter Collection's Dave Lees (left) and pilot Lee Proudfoot (standing, right) during preparations for the first flight of LF Mk XVIE TB863/G-CDAN. Lees is one of TFC's Spitfire airframe engineers, and is currently working on the Collection's ex-Indian Air Force FR Mk XIV MV293/G-SPIT

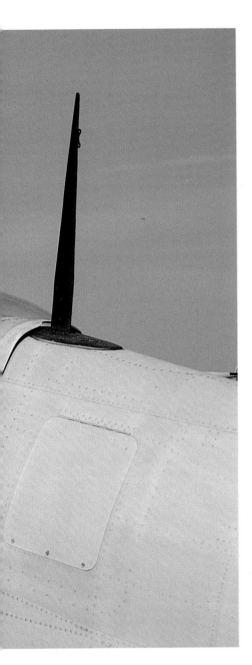

Below No, he's not wondering where to start. Dick Melton knows his way around a Spitfire's innards better than most. Trained as an engineering apprentice at RAF Halton in the late 1950s, Dick worked on piston-engined transports in various parts of the world until posted to RAF Chivenor in Devon, where he was entrusted with the care of the DH Mosquitoes serving with 3 CAACU at Exeter Airport, and later employed in filming *633 Squadron*. A spell at RAF St Mawgan servicing Shackleton maritime patrol aircraft led to an eight-year stint with the Battle of Britain Memorial Flight, further strengthening his intimate knowledge of Merlins and Griffons. Since retirement from the RAF Dick Melton has worked for Doug Arnold's Warbirds of Great Britain collection when it was based at Blackbushe Airport, and in 1984 he joined the late Charles Church at nearby Roundwood, near Micheldever, to help him realise his dream of rebuilding and flying his own fleet of Spitfires. Since Church's death in July 1989, Dick has set up his own company, Dick Melton Aviation, to restore and maintain the Charles Church (Spitfires) Ltd fleet at Roundwood, as well as restoring a Supermarine Walrus biplane amphibian as a personal project. As if that weren't enough to keep him busy, Dick also has a contract to perform a Major Servicing on one of the BBMF's PR Mk XIXs

Pete Rushen is seen here refuelling and in the rear cockpit of Carolyn Grace's Tr9 ML407, is a former 'Halton Brat' and ex-BBMF engineer with many post-service years of experience working on privately-owned Spitfires. Chief Engineer with The Fighter Collection at Duxford for many years, Pete had never flown in the type with which he has been associated for much of his career until he became the newly checked-out Carolyn Grace's first (and clearly delighted) passenger

Who are these people, and why are they smiling? They are a unique trio of lady Spitfire pilots (left to right): Joan Hughes, MBE; Carolyn Grace, and Lettice Curtis. Joan and Lettice were members of the Air Transport Auxiliary, the wartime ferry pilot pool whose many young lady fliers, mostly recruited from pre-war civilian flying clubs, collected new aircraft from manufacturers and flew them across country on delivery to RAF squadrons and maintenance units. Armed with nothing more than a set of Pilot's Notes, they were called upon to fly, single-handed, anything from docile trainers to high-performance fighters and four-engined bombers. Spitfires figure prominently in the logbook of Joan Hughes and even more so in that of Lettice Curtis, who, after ATA service, flew Warbirds of Great Britain's PR Mk XI PL983 (see page 94) when it was the personal aircraft of the American Air Attaché to the US Embassy in London, and set several air racing records in it. Home base to peripatetic ATA pilots was White Waltham Airfield, near Maidenhead, where this picture was taken in September 1991 during a gathering of women pilots young and not so young. And the smiles? Whether your last Spitfire flight was half an hour or nearly half a century ago, you smile at the memory

Susanna Church, about to fly in the back seat of her late husband Charles's Tr9 PT462/G-CTIX. Obsessed with Spitfires since he was eight years old, property developer Church learned to fly but quickly discovered that airworthy Spitfires were not readily available, so he and Dick Melton set about recovering non-flying airframes and rebuilding them. Having trained and soloed on PT462, and just obtained his Basic Commercial Pilot's Licence, he was tragically killed in July 1989 while attempting to forced-land his single-seat Spitfire LF Mk VC EE606/G-MKVC following a catastrophic crankshaft failure. His widow is continuing the collection to perpetuate his memory